Michi~~gan~~

MW00618522

2

Be Safe
Ron

by

Ron Rademacher

Revised Edition

Back Roads Publication

6960 Lakeview Dr.

Bellevue, Michigan 49021

TABLE OF CONTENTS

Michigan Back Roads
2

by

Ron Rademacher

Back Roads Publication

6960 Lakeview Dr.

Bellevue, Michigan 49021

Acknowledgments

No book is the work of just one person. This one wouldn't have been written without the unwavering support and excellent proofreading by Terry Mulvaney and Tabitha.

Cover Illustration by Terry Mulvaney

Special thanks are due to all the folks in the small Michigan towns who have made time for my presentations, endless questions and photographic intrusions.

Michigan Back Roads
2
by Ron Rademacher

Published by
Back Roads Publications
6960 Lakeview Dr.
Bellevue, Michigan 49021

Copyright 2009 by Ron Rademacher
Revised Edition 2013
ISBN 1-57166-585-4

EXPERIENCE STURGIS – FESTIVAL

A bit of history:

The Great Sauk Trail was the main stage route from Detroit to Chicago for pioneers heading west. Whether to open up the far west or as a jumping off point for folks headed "up north" in Michigan, this route, now U.S. 12, was the northern frontier well into the late 1800's. The Sauk Trail intersected the Nottawaseepe Trail, an indian route, at this point when the first settlers arrived around 1827. The towns and villages are full of stories, legends, and historic sites. Sturgis Michigan has created an entire festival dedicated to embracing and preserving this history. A rich history was made here, for example, the corner of South Monroe St. once was a Free Church that welcomed those preachers who had fallen out of favor with the orthodoxy of their own churches; it became a Spiritualist headquarters and was the first place a motion picture was shown in Sturgis. Then there was the 16 acres of terraces, gardens and streams known as Oaklawn Terrace. The area had been a dumping ground but was transformed by unemployed working men to pay off their light and water bills. There was the Old Sturgis Inn where notable travelers rested along the Fort

Dearborn - Detroit Highway. Always on the move, Sturgis became known as the "Electric City" because they built one of the first hydro-electric dams in the region.

The Festival:

While you will find a lot of activities that other festivals offer, you are going to discover Sturgis in a whole new way and experience the tapestry of 150+ years of a Michigan town on the frontier. The festival is usually in October,

Much of the architecture and events of historic Sturgis have been preserved. Every year the town pays tribute to history and recreates the environment and atmosphere of 150 years ago. Townspeople dress in period garb and the streets are lit to enhance the experience. You can stroll along the Chicago Road and tour the historic buildings, many of which have been marked with informative plaques and tour bank buildings, law offices, and an early electric shop. You can still go into the building that was Tribbett's, a store that was opened in 1904 as a five and dime. Lowry's Books is there today, only the second business to occupy this spot.

Businesses and shops have displays of old photographs, vintage appliances and apparel, classic cars and tons of local history. There are arts and crafts including Master Wood Carvers, Silversmithing and Pioneer Skills. How about a pancake breakfast to start, a free movie, tours of the Historical Museum, a real shoe cobbler, making electricity and all of the tours of historic churches and other structures you could ask for.

Directions:

Sturgis is at the crossroads of the Sauk Trail (US 12) & Route 66 in southern most Michigan.

Side trips:

Colon – The Magic Capital

White Pigeon – Just a few miles west of Sturgis, this small town is home to an awesome nut house; they roast their own. It is at the main intersection.

DID YOU KNOW?

IN THE EARLY DAYS

STURGIS

WAS KNOWN

AS

THE

ELECTRIC CITY

MICHIGAN'S BOOT HILL CEMETERY

A bit of history:

It is true. Michigan does have an old cemetery that was known as Boot Hill. While it didn't become as famous as the one out west, it did become the final resting place of some of the most famous, infamous and colorful characters who ever lived during the great lumber days of the 1880's and the 1890's. Schoolcraft county is in the central part of the upper peninsula and the central part of the county is mostly uninhabited. A large section is dedicated to the Seney wildlife preserve. On the eastern edge is the town of Seney and while most folks today go ripping through on their way somewhere else, there is great history in this tiny crossroads.

During those rip-roaring years, this was one of the toughest and roughest towns in the world. Tales are told of the fights, robberies and killings that greeted the traveler. Characters like Leon Czolgosz, who later assassinated President McKinley and P.J. "Snap Jaw" Small who earned his whiskey by biting off the heads of living snakes and frogs. He made it to "Michigan's Boot Hill" after biting off the head of another lumberjack's pet owl. There was "Pump Handle Joe" and "Protestant Bob" McGuire and "Stub Foot" O'Donnell, bar room brawlers of the most murderous sort.

What you will find:

If you head straight south of town for a mile or so, you will come to the old cemetery, "Michigan's Boot Hill". Lots of these fellas and many others were buried there. Most of the graves are still there but only one or two markers have survived the passing years. Many were buried with no records kept at all. You can learn about those days by visiting the local historical museum open all summer long. They have lots of artifacts and old records. You can find out about "Wiry" Jim Summers, "Frying Pan Mag" and more.

Directions:

The village of Seney is at the junction of 77 and 28. The cemetery and the historical museum are just south of 28.

Side trips:

While much of Schoolcraft County is spectacular, the drive west from here on M-28 is considered one of the most boring in Michigan. From Seney west to Shingleton is more than 30 miles of flat, featureless two-lane road. It is easy to overlook the towns and history here and the fact that you are on the edge of one of our great wilderness preserves.

If you continue on west, you will be following the same route the lumberjacks did as they followed the pine. After them came the miners. One of the famous old lumbermen who didn't end up in the Boot Hill at Seney was "Silver Jack" Driscoll. His legend is large from the Tittabawassee River all the way to the Huron Mountains, and it is in those mountains where he claimed to have found a gold mine. After 1893 "Silver Jack" spent his last days in L'Anse fighting, drinking and brawling as always. When he ran out of money, he would head north into the Huron Mountains, a trackless wilderness that is still one of the most remote areas in Michigan. "Silver Jack" would reappear after a couple of weeks resupplied with gold nuggets and sometimes silver. He would hang around the saloons until he was broke and head out again. Concerned citizens tried to track him into the mountains no doubt concerned that he would twist an ankle or get mauled by a bear and need help, but he would always elude them. Soon he would be back with more nuggets. He never divulged the location of his mine and the secret of its location is now lost, just like "Silver Jack"s" final resting place.

A PALACE – A FICKLE HEART

The Story:

In the 1880's Robert Richardi, a German immigrant, built a factory in Bellaire, Michigan to produce wooden ware, some based on his own patents. The factory was extremely modern for the times and ran on power produced from a dam on the nearby river. They made high quality wooden kitchen utensils for the most part. At one time the factory employed more than 140 people. In 1890 the factory burned down and Robert decided to leave the area. He left the company to his son Henri.

Henri continued to work in the area and wanted to get started on a family. He asked his German girlfriend to marry him but she was hesitant to move to the northern wilderness from her home in Germany. Henri persisted and promised to build her the most beautiful house in the state if she would marry him. The lady told him to build the house first and then she would come to America and marry him. He got right to work.

Henri Richardi proceeded to build a Victorian style house the likes of which had never been seen in the wild lumber country. Nothing was considered to good for his bride-to-be. The rooms were paneled with fine hardwoods, there was indoor plumbing, a central heating system and electric lights; amenities unheard of at the time. The claim could be made that this was the country's first electric home and it was run from the hydroelectric dam at the river. Fireplaces with carved mantels, hardwood pocket doors and beautiful wall paper all combined to produce a spectacular interior. The exterior is just as stunning. After years of work the labor of love was complete. Henri sent photos of the incredible home to his girlfriend. Alas, she declined to be impressed and refused to leave home and marry him. Broken-hearted he boarded up the house and never even lived in it.

What you will find:

The house is still there today and is considered one of the top examples of Queen Anne architecture in the entire country. What is more is that you can not only tour the house, you can stay there. It is now a Bed and Breakfast, the Grand Victorian. Many of the original details have been preserved including much of the hand crafted woodwork, the likes of which we probably won't see produced again.

Directions:

The Grand Victorian is on the edge of downtown Bellaire, Michigan. Trust me, you can't miss it. Bellaire is in Antrim County in the northwest of Michigan just east of Torch Lake on Route 88.

Side Trips:

There are so many things to do that I could write an entire book about day trips in this region. So, here are a few nearby treasures that will be sure to please.

The Bellaire Historical Museum is downtown and houses a rich collection of photos and artifacts from the period during which the house was built.

Torch Lake is regarded as one of the most beautiful lakes in the world. The indescribable hues of blue and turquoise have baffled poets and painters for two centuries.

Elk Rapids is a favorite shopping destination, but those in the know don't overlook the unique shops in Alden.

A few miles south is Rapid City and one of the roads leading out of Rapid City is the Valley

Road. A few miles along the way is a tiny spot to pull off. That spot leads to the 7 Bridges Nature Area.

You may want to dine while in the area. Lulu's in Bellaire is not to be missed.

THE HUMUNGUS FUNGUS FESTIVAL

The Story:

Mushrooms growing up through a tree stump turn out to be just the tip of the proverbial iceberg.   In 1988 in the forest near Crystal Falls, Michigan, they discovered what at the time was the largest and oldest living organism on earth, Armillaria bulbosa; a giant fungus. When I say giant I mean it, 30+ acres at last measurement, It is estimated that, if you could pull the whole thing up, it would weigh more than 100 tons.

The Festival:

Every August they get it going in Crystal Falls to celebrate fungus. Why not? For four days it is nothing but fun and games. You can tube down the Paint River, enter a cribbage tournament, enjoy the Fungus Fest Parade or compete in the Horse Pull.

Pasties are a dietary staple and there are plenty to try but don't forget; this town has the best smoked bratwurst available in Michigan. Then there is the Car Cruise, the craft show, the volleyball tournament and tons of stuff for the kids. Try not to miss the Finn vs Pollack Softball Games, men's and women's.

There is even more and this is one gorgeous town to spend a weekend in.

Directions:

The Festival events take place all over town. One of the main check in spots is Runkle Park on the east side of town and it is great for camping.

Crystal Falls is in the upper peninsula a few miles north of the Split Rock.

Side Trips:

Horse Race Rapids is just south of town. The climb down to the river is a bit rough but well worth it, especially if the white water kayakers are in action.

THE CHESANING BRIDGE DISASTER

The Story:

Not all historic events took place long, long ago. In the winters of 2008 and again in 2009, the Shiawassee River at Chesaning demonstrated the awesome power of Michigan winters. Chesaning, Michigan is an historic town located in the center of Saginaw County on the banks of the Shiawassee River and the history of town and river have been linked since the area was first settled. This community has long taken genuine interest in preserving local history and it was with great pride that they purchased a trestle bridge that was slated for demolition from a nearby town. At great expense the entire structure was moved to the River Front Park that borders downtown and was installed on foundations just downstream from the dam to link the foot path on each bank.

Everyone applauded the spirit of preservation and agreed that the bridge, one of only three in the U.S., was a genuine treasure and a crown jewel of the foot path. The whole community was set to enjoy the picturesque bridge crossing that was so unique to the town and park. As autumn came to an end and winter approached, no one anticipated that it would be any different from any other, nor the amazing event that was about to take place.

The river froze which was not that unusual. Ice began to build up and push on the old dam. This was no great concern since the town was planning to demolish the dam and replace it with a modern weir anyway. If the ice build up helped that process, so much the better but, there was trouble coming as Mother Nature rolled up her sleeves, spit on her hands and got down to it. The ice continued to build up and stack up and stack up some more until it was high enough to reach the bridge which was way up in the air, I mean way up. Then, incredibly, the ice lifted the newly moved bridge right off its foundations. The weather got colder and the ice kept coming and finally the river won. The beautiful historic bridge was dumped into the river and was completely wrecked.

What you'll find:

At this writing the old dam is being replaced with a modern weir that will produce super rapids that will be the delight of kayakers and canoers. At the same spot is a new restaurant that will have riverside dining and WiFi. The River Front Park continues to develop and all of this is just downstream from Showboat Park. The old wrecked bridge is still in the river and kids love playing on it but it is scheduled to be removed.

Directions:

Chesaning, Michigan, is an hour and half northeast of Detroit on Route 57. The river flows right through downtown.

Side Trips:

A visit to the Chesaning Historical Museum will be worth the effort. They have photos of how the bridge was brought to town and installed.

The Bonnymill Inn is close to everything in town and is worth a tour even if you can't stay.

For river enthusiasts, the park offers camping right on the river.

DID YOU KNOW?

THE WORD CHESANING

COMES FROM A

NATIVE AMERICAN WORD

MEANING

PLACE OF THE

BIG ROCK

THE GINGERBREAD FESTIVAL

The Event:

The first weekend in December an entire town becomes a Gingerbread Village and they do it up right. This is a real old-fashioned holiday...where true happiness is homemade. In fact, there is nothing like the spicy aroma of gingerbread baking on a frosty winter's day. Caro, Michigan, is transformed for an entire week. There are concerts, a bake goods contest (featuring gingerbread), live reindeer, parades, lights, storytelling, tea and lots of photo ops.

What you will find:

When you get to town, you could head for Gingerbread central and get a schedule of events. The store windows are decorated; there are gingerbread cookies and cakes and treats. The proceedings are overseen by your hosts Fred and Ginger Bread, the king and queen of the Gingerbread Village. You can take part in the Holiday Home Tour, the Family Fun Trail Walk or any of the Make-n-Take Activities that are available for children.

You can also get great recipes for gingerbread, directions for creating an edible gingerbread house or you can just wander the streets and enjoy the treats. There really isn't another festival quite like this one. You will hardly believe the intricate gingerbread houses the local artists create.

Directions:

Caro, Michigan, is in the upper part of the "thumb" of the lower peninsula and is only about an hour and a half north of Detroit, an easy day trip. The village is at the junction of 24 and 81 about 30 miles east of Saginaw. More information is available on the Michigan Back Roads web site and on the Caro Chamber of Commerce web site.

Side Trips:

Just one hint – J.J. Jamokes and deep fried dill pickles – it is worth it. I can't wait to have some more.

HIDDEN FALLS – LOWER PENNINSULA

The Trip:

There are tons of waterfalls in the upper peninsula of Michigan. Some folks think there is just one in the lower peninsula and some folks swear there are two. In fact, there are at least three waterfalls in the lower peninsula of Michigan. To visit this unnamed waterfall you have to drive into the heart of the Manistee National Forest. You are going to take a couple of gravel roads and then a gorgeous walk to the falls that cascades into the Manistee River. You can picnic or camp on a bluff overlooking the falls and the river. It is important to note that the trail to the falls is a bit rough and quite steep in places so dress appropriately, especially if you go in winter.

What you will find:

After following the first directions below, you will be at the Hodenpyl Dam. You could cross the river at this spot on a very cool suspension foot bridge and get to the North Country Trail. The dam creates the Hodenpyl Pond, and the falls are downstream a couple of miles from here. Now you make the decision to walk along the trails or drive further into the forest as described in the second directions.

Directions:

First directions: Get onto Route 37. This is an excellent paved two lane that intersects 10 in Baldwin. Head out of Baldwin and make for Mesick about 30 miles north. A few miles south of Mesick you want to take NO 26 RD and head west. This is gravel so go easy as it can be a bit rough. Stay on the road and follow it around as it curves to the right. There are other roads branching off, but if you stay on this, you will get to the dam and parking area. Now you park and walk or take the second part of the drive.

Second directions: From the dam turn left onto the two track "snake trail" that heads into the forest, go slow. This two track will branch often and every time it does you want to keep to the right. Keep going and branching right and after a while you will see a metal gate on your right. The last time I was there it was painted brown. This is the first gate you will have come to.

Park in any of the rough parking spots, there are 4 or 5 and walk around the gate. Go back to your car and get your camera. Walk around the gate.

Go back to your car and get your picnic basket. Walk around the gate. The trail starts here and in a few moments you will hear only the birds and the wind in the trees. 600 – 700 yards down the trail you will arrive at river and the falls.

Waterfall notes:

There are, in fact, two other waterfalls in the lower peninsula. One is Ocqueoc Falls in Presque Isle County. Another is in southwest Michigan. It is in an unusual cave that played a part in a bank robbery back in the 1800's. Yet another seasonal fall spills into the Au Sable next to the "Stairway to Heaven".

Falls Illustration by Amy Fox

HIDDEN FALLS - UPPER PENINSULA

The Trip:

This is an easy relaxing drive that will take you to five waterfalls in one afternoon. The falls include Wagner Falls, Scott Falls, Laughing Whitefish Falls, Alger Falls and a small waterfall that isn't on any map I know of. A couple of the falls can be seen without getting out of your car and all of them are very accessible. There are a number of ways to take this drive depending on your starting point. I am kind of an "old Michigan" guy so we started from the Gladstone Motel. There are picnic spots on this trip.

Drive Options:

Starting from Gladstone, we went north on 41 to Trenary where you catch 67 going north. A few miles on and you will come to 94 where you will turn right. Remember this junction because the **secret waterfall** is nearby and we will be coming back this way. Just 16 miles further and you come to Highway 28 near Munising. Alger Falls is at that junction. Turn around, head back and park at the pull off. A short stroll up a well tended path will bring you to Wagner Falls, a beautiful falls that fills the air with music.

After a few minutes at the waterfall, you will want to dash back to your car and start reading this swell book again. Head toward Munising. The road pretty much follows the shore of Lake Superior and you can see Grand Island in the distance. Stay on 28 for a few miles and just west of Munising is Scott Falls on the left. On the right side of the road is a park where you can stop and take pictures. Continuing west watch for a road named H-03 near Au Train where you will turn left. This is an improved road, but take it slow, allow yourself to enjoy the gorgeous forest. You could have turned right, but it is very wet that way. Keep heading south on H-03 for 4 or 5 miles and you will arrive back at 94. Go west, that is a right turn, and in 4 miles you will be at the junction of 94 & 67 again; the junction I said you should remember. Turn right, that is north, and drive toward Chatham. Go easy since you will pull off the road quite soon.

Rolling north toward Chatham you will see a rather small municipal park on the left-hand side of the road. There is an enormous snow-roller there, pictured in Michigan Back Roads 1, and a couple of one-holers for the convenience of travelers and those on a picnic. In fact, this is one of the great spots for a picnic on this drive. The park is enclosed by a split rail fence and at the back of the park is an archway with a path leading into the trees. Down that path a bit you will come to a small waterfall that isn't on any map. It is in a small clearing about a five minute walk in and you will hear it before you see it. No, it isn't a thundering cataract like Canyon Falls, but it is a tranquil spot visited by few.

Back on the road, you head north into Chatham and follow 94 west again. Seven miles down the road you will come to Sundell, Michigan. Watch for the sign telling you to turn north to reach Laughing Whitefish Falls. This is a famous waterfall, and it is only a couple of miles to the parking area. The road was a bit dicey last time I went. After parking you will have to walk about a mile but the path is not bad, and the waterfall is worth every step of it. We explored for an hour and had a great time; no one else was there.

We are in the car again and are back at 94 heading west again. In about 7 miles you will come to 41 again. If you turn south here, you will be back in Gladstone in less than an hour.

Side Trips:

After Laughing White Fish Falls you reach the junction of 94 & 41. If you turn north instead, there is a very pretty drive. Follow 94 as it meanders north and west until you come to 553. Take 553 south about 5 miles and you will come to 35. Turn right toward Gwinn and stay on 35 for about 15 miles. The road twists and turns all over so drive carefully. Up towards Palmer you will find Warner Falls which can be seen from the road. A bit further on is the National Mine near Ishpeming. You have to see the site to believe it. When you have had enough just follow 35 south and you will get back to Gladstone.

Trenary Toast:

Early in our trip we passed by Trenary. A tiny village noted for Outhouse Races and murals. Also in town is the bakery that makes Trenary Toast. Ask around at the small markets you find. Packaged in brown paper bags this stuff is incredible, especially if you dunk it in coffee for breakfast.

NAHMA – 3 DAY GETAWAY

Nahma:

Nahma, Michigan is one of those hidden gems that the travels love to find. On the shore of Lake Michigan in the upper peninsula, this is a beautiful quiet place where you are only a stranger when you first arrive. After that you are a friend who is made welcome whether you are there for the bird watching, the Nahma Music Festival, or are planning to spend a couple days and enjoy the day trips. When you leave, you will be refreshed and will take wonderful memories away with you.

There are three roads that lead into town and each is a scenic drive worth seeing. The town is very small but offers an artists gallery, a golf course, fishing, parks and a hiking trail and the unique Nahma Inn. Everyone who comes to Nahma eventually visits the inn where the people are friendly and the food is great. The Nahma Inn offers lodging that is a step back in time. All rooms is on the second floor which is reached by stairs. The venue is from a simpler time with small clean rooms, some with private restrooms and some and shared baths. Guests gather in the dining room or tavern for conversation and to enjoy the impromptu musical performances that are liable to break out at any time.

Nahma Township is a sportsman's fantasy. The abundance of water, open public land and wildlife create a condition for fisherman, hunters, trappers, boaters, kayakers, off road riders, hikers and all outdoorsman where many sporting opportunities can be undertaken all in the same area.

Day 1 – Nahma Marsh Trail:

This 0.3 mile linear trail once crept under a dense cedar forest, but a windstorm in 1997 leveled the trees leaving hikers today with broad vistas of the marsh. This hard surfaced fully accessible trail ends at a two-tiered viewing platform where an assortment of wetland wildlife can be seen. Rest areas with benches are space every 200 feet or so along the trail. This is an easy trail near the Sturgeon River in the Hiawatha National Forest. Ruffled Grouse, whitetail deer and sandhill cranes are just a few of the native wildlife you may encounter.

Day 2 – Eben Ice Caves – Winter:

The Rock River Canyon Ice Caves, also known as the Eben Ice Caves, are a unique destination for a winter day trip. While this beautiful natural wonder is being visited more often, many people have still never heard of it. The Rock River Wilderness area includes over 4,000 acres in the Hiawatha National Forest. The ice caves are high on the wall of the river gorge with ice formations as much as sixty feet tall.

When you arrive at the parking area you will find minimal facilities so take your water and energy bars with you. In fact, on a week day you may be the only people there. The first part of the hike is easy going across a farm field. The second part is pretty easy as well, through the woodlands toward the river gorge. About half way there you will come to a sign describing the area and pointing out that the trail into the gorge is steep, slippery and possibly treacherous; believe it.

The final part of the hike is into the gorge with steep up and down sections. It is snow covered, with wet rocks and icy conditions. When you reach the bottom of the river gorge you still have a short hike along the waterway. Then you will have a short steep climb up to the caves. The hike is over a mile all told and is worth every bit of it. The giant ice formation looks like a frozen waterfall. You can actually walk inside the cavern and experience the light coming through a curtain of ice.

Directions: From the Nahma Inn you travel north on 41 to Trenary and take 67 north to Chatham. Take 94 west to Eben Junction and follow the little signs to the ice caves.

Day 3 – 5 Waterfalls Scenic Drive

See chapter on the Hidden Waterfall on page 25

Directions to Nahma: Nahma is on the shore of Big Bay de Noc between Escanaba and Manistique. Travel U.S. 2 ontil you come to Nahma Junction. Drive south 5 miles to Nahma.

AN ODDITY IN NEWBERRY

The Story:

In 1896 a tremendous wind storm swept across the upper peninsula. One of the trees the storm blew over was on the farm of John McGuer. According to the Soo Evening News several mysterious objects were stuck in the root system of an enormous old hemlock felled by that storm. The items included 3 statues and a large stone tablet. The tablet was engraved with strange inscriptions.

The largest statue was nearly life size and seems to depict a man sitting on a sort of pedestal. The second appeared to be a woman and is a bit smaller. The third and smallest statue seems to be the image of a child. All three are of sandstone and had the appearance of great age. The tablet, found nearby, was about 18" by 25". One side was covered with 140 inscriptions engraved in rows. Each row was made up of squares about 1 ½ inches in size.

For many weeks after the discovery, these odd artifacts were on display in a store in Newberry. While speculation ran wild, no one then or now has come up with an answer to the question of origin. Nor has anyone ever satisfactorily produced a coherent translation of the tablet inscriptions. Photos were submitted to universities, scholars and experts and were pretty much poo – pooed although excellent photos were taken by the Smithsonian and were published in Issue 71 of Ancient American.

Eventually, the furor died down and the four pieces were stored away in the McGruer barn and suffered a lot of damage through the years. Sometime around 1929 the remnants were gathered up and moved to a small museum at Fort Algonquin where they were stored away under the stairs and were pretty much forgotten except by the occasional searcher.

What you will find:

Unlike many stories about mysterious artifacts, some of these objects are still around. The tablet has been lost completely but excellent photos and drawings of it are on display. Likewise, the statues are very much the worse for wear but parts do exist and are on display but not in Newberry. Photos, reprints and attempted translations await anyone who is curious and can be seen at the Fort de Buade Indian Museum in St. Ignace. The museum is operated by the local historical society and has over 6000 square feet on exhibits.

Directions:

The museum is on 334 N. State Street in downtown St. Ignace and is open May 30 – October 1.

Side Note:

There is a translation of the Newberry Stone Tablet by Barry Fell. His position is that the tablet depicts a magic quadrangle and should be read both vertically and horizontally in alternate directions. He further purported that these magical charms were probably copies of something from the eastern Mediterranean. I am not aware of any explanation for how they got here. The translation is a bit cryptic as one would expect and is on display at the museum as well.

KRUZZIN' KLASSICS FUN RUN

The Festival:

Cars, baby, that is the main story. The classic cars come rolling into town on Friday night, and there are big doings at the Fair Grounds on the north edge of town. The car rally is just the beginning. During the weekend there will be street dancing and a classic car will be given away.

You want to plan carefully because you don't want to miss the Rib Cook Off. You don't have to take my word for it, but this is no ordinary Rib Fest. Just ask the 600 people who chowed down in 2008 and the folks who didn't plan very well and missed out; incredible ribs.

What you will find:

Downtown Escanaba is graced by one of the loveliest historic boulevards in Michigan. Historic architecture lines the street and historic vehicles will add to the fun. There are some genuine treasures here. Bonifas Arts Center is a jewel and the Sand Point Lighthouse is one of the most accessible in the U.P.

Directions:

Go north across "the bridge" and head west on U.S. 2. If coming from Wisconsin or Utah or someplace, head east on U.S. 2.

Side Trips:

You want local color? Eat breakfast at Rosie's Diner. It isn't the only place but it is unique.

Fishing is an obligation and the pier in Gladstone makes it just too much fun.

H-63 A REAL "OLD MICHIGAN" DRIVE

The Trip:

You cross the bridge over the Straits of Mackinac and I-75 will take you north to Sault Ste. Marie or 2 will send you west to Manistique, Gladstone and on to Felch. If you are going north, you might consider going on the old road.

What you will find:

H-63 is a two-lane paved road that runs from St. Ignace to Sault Ste. Marie. At one time back when the ferry was the only way across the Straits, it was the only road to the "Soo". Even though you are only a few yards from I-75 which runs on a nearly parallel course, if you drive both of these, you would swear these roads are in different worlds. The highway is the highway and you rush along with everyone else in a hurry to get there. H-63, the old Mackinac Trail, winds along the same course but is surrounded by evergreen trees and not much else. If you go in the winter, about the only thing you are liable to encounter is a deer or a snowmobile and gently falling snowflakes.

You pass through historic Rudyard and Kinross, site of a famous UFO chase, within a few miles of Brimley and finally into Sault Ste. Marie, the third oldest town in the United States.

Directions:

After you cross "The Bridge," continue north until you reach the second St. Ignace Exit. At the stop, turn toward town and follow the sign to the Mackinac Trail. Pick up H-63, head north and enjoy the ride.

Side Trips:

Castle Rock – is at the exit where you get off the interstate and was once a lookout point for Native Americans, French trappers and others. You can still climb to the top and on a clear day, you can see the Pines Motel.

PIGS FIND A FORTUNE

The Story:

Up on the Keweenaw Peninsula, copper country, legends abound about fortunes lost and found. Some say that the famous Calumet Conglomerate was discovered, or rediscovered, because some pigs made a break for the wide open-spaces.

Back in the 1800's Ed Hulbert ran a boarding house called the Half Way House. One night it seems that some folks came looking for help to find some runaway pigs. The story goes that the pigs evaded the searchers that night, but when the search began again the next morning, some searchers said they could hear pigs snuffling around and the sound seemed to come from under ground. After scouring the crags and underbrush, a large pit was found and, sure enough, there were the pigs rooting around happy as, well, pigs in a mud hole.

That pit contained rubble, tailings and pre-historic stone tools. A further search eventually led to the discovery of the Calumet Conglomerate, a copper lode that was 35 miles long. A mining company was established which became the Calumet and

Hecla, millions of pounds of copper were recovered and Calumet grew into one of the jewels of Keweenaw Peninsula.

What you will find:

A visit to Calumet should be on every itinerary that takes you to the western upper peninsula. Downtown is a National Historic Landmark District. St. Ann's Church is one of the most beautiful in copper country. The Calumet Theatre is a National Historic Landmark and, in my opinion, is one of the two most beautiful in Michigan.

The Coppertown Mining Museum is excellent. Rock hounds love the area because of the variety which includes agates, copper, datolite and greenstones. There is still much to discover here.

Directions:

The Hecla buildings are in downtown Calumet just off U.S. 41.

Side trips:

There are enough side trips to keep you right here for weeks. One of my favorites is Cliff. About 14 miles further north from Calumet is the town of

Phoenix. About 3 or 4 miles before you get there is a small sign by the side of the road that simply says "Cliff Cemetery". If it is safe to do so, pull off and follow the old path into the forest. After a short way, you will be in the old cemetery that served the town of Clifton. After your visit, continue north and you will find the old ghost town, now a museum complex.

While not discovered by pigs, this was the Keweenaw's first profitable mine eventually producing 40 million pounds of copper. This is rough country; and in the 1800's, the conditions were harsh at best. Tough people came here and wrested a living from the rocks. Their story is told by the stones in the cemetery at the bottom of the cliff.

DID YOU KNOW?

THE PASTY IS A

CORNISH INVENTION

AND WAS A STAPLE

FOR MINERS.

AMASA PIKE FEST

The Festival:

The Pike Fest is held every year in Amasa, Michigan, and it is another very cool winter festival. Quickly becoming a favorite of the locals and fisher-folk from all over, the event is held the day before the Super Bowl. There are prizes for the biggest Northern Pike and for the biggest Walleye Pike. In 2008, the winning Northern was 34" and the Walleye was 23". There were more than 100 participants.

This is a hook and line tournament only, no spearing. Fish must be caught the day of the event and must be taken from Iron County waters. At the end of the day there is a full banquet served and live music. A lot of fun. Even if you don't compete in the fishing you can compete in the story telling.

What you will find:

Amasa is a tiny village on the Hemlock River in central Iron County. The old train depot is there, and there is an excellent historical museum. Headquarters for the Festival is at the Rusty Sawblade Tavern & Grill in downtown Amasa.

Everything you need is there; you can even get a room for the night with WiFi.

You can contact the Rusty Sawblade through my website

Directions:

The only sure way to get to Amasa is on Route 141, between U.S. 2 and Route 28. Plan ahead, folks, this is January in the upper peninsula, and it has been known to snow that time of year.

Side Trips:

This time of year almost any direction you go in is going to be an adventure. The snow mobile-riders can give you lots of tips. I would head for the Park View Lodge in Twin Lakes for liver and onions but if you don't have the time then get some of the pasties around at Granny T's on the road between Ishpeming and Negaunee.

RIDE THE BREEZEWAY

The Trip:

The journey is the thing; not how fast you can get from here to there or how fast you can get settled in; the ride is the joy and the fun. The BREEZEWAY is as cool a ride as you will find in any part of Michigan. Twenty Five miles plus is what you have and it is inviting for all kinds of vehicles, bikes, motorcycles, cars and just plain hiking. Access is easy and you can get there from U.S. 31 or from U.S. 131, the main ride is on C-48. Keep in mind though, there are treasures in the drumlins; north and south of "The Breezeway".

What you will find:

C-48 – just another county road. C – 48 runs from Atwood on the west end to Boyne Falls on the east end. Smack dab in the middle is East Jordan at the southern extreme of Lake Charlevoix. A drive of approximately 25 miles through drop-dead gorgeous Michigan. The drive is through rolling hills and stunning vistas on a single two-lane paved road, and it doesn't matter at which end you start. The drumlins, (drumlins are rare glacial hill formations), make this a one of a kind drive in Michigan and my advice is to go one way, then turn around and go back the other way. Be prepared to be delighted all over again. The whole thing is simply breathtaking, and that is just the scenery.

See, there are quaint towns that are so lovely if you google the phrase "quaint town in Michigan", one of these is probably pictured there. You can approach East Jordan from any direction and find yourself gasping at how picturesque and dang "quaint" it is. All along the way are reasons to stop and have fun. There is the soap-making shop and the fishing and the burger place, and the antique shops and the farmers' markets and the glass blower and, ya know, fun; and that is just in the summer. You won't even believe this ride during color tour time.

Side Trips:

The "Breezeway" runs pretty much east and west. You can spend a couple days exploring the main road and the towns on it. There are, however, a couple of treasures that are worth the time.

Jordan Valley Glassworks is in East Jordan. A simple block building with a simple display outside. Inside are some of the most talented glassblower/artists in the U.S. If you don't stop here, well....

The Ironton Ferry – just a few miles north on 66 you hit the main body of Lake Charlevoix. At this point is the small town of Ironton and the Ironton Ferry operates here. The car ferry will hold maybe four cars and the crossing lasts about 10 minutes. Then you are on the south end of Lake Charlevoix and can explore from there; I recommend Horton Bay and the Horton Creek Inn.

You can go wild on side trips here. The Central Lakes Iron Works, The Blue Pelican Inn, Soaps N' Such, Raven Hill Discovery Center and on and on.

Remember – The National Morel Mushroom Festival in May.

Alice and a Humungus Fungus by Dawn Baumer

SAILOR PINES – A VIRGIN FOREST

The Trip:

You can still take a walk through our natural heritage in the lower peninsula. The last wave of the lumber era was passing in the 1920's in mid-Michigan. At the same time, Mr. William Sailors began to review his timberland holdings in Newaygo County. He discovered that he had several acres of white pine that were maturing but were not yet large enough for harvesting. He had participated in the lumber boom and had seen the fantastic giant pines toppled forest by forest. After that, the hardwoods were harvested and the land was cleared of the wonderous old trees. But not all of it. While dealing in hardwoods, Mr. Sailors discovered a neglected stand of white pines and decided to preserve them. His son, David, carried on this work and the result is a stand of virgin pine that is a quiet place available to all. James Sailors is the current owner and the pines have matured to a point similar to what lumberjacks would have found in the 1800's.

What you will find:

You can pull into the trees and park. You can walk just a few yards in and will be surrounded by enormous old Michigan white pine trees. Many are more than 30" in diameter and several are more than 100' tall. Wander along the path for a bit longer and feel yourself transported to a quieter time and a less-hurried pace. If you bring a picnic lunch, you can pause long enough for your inner self to slow down and become quiet enough to hear the winds whispering in the pines, hear deer walking nearby and glimpse wild turkeys foraging. All of this is just a few minutes from town and easily accessible by car. The road going to the pines is even paved. Sailors Pines are easy to get to at any time of day, but the solitude is truly amazing place at sunrise.

You are welcome here and can bring a lunch; however, no camping is allowed and NO FIRES.

Directions:

The short version is that the pines are located at 52nd Street, 1/4 mile east of Locust Ave. From Newaygo, go north across the river and go east on Croton Dr. Just before you reach the dam turn north on Pear Ave. After a couple of miles, you will hit 52nd. Go right, jog left and then right again and you will find the Pines.

Side Trips:

The Croton – Hardy Dam is a very popular destination with plenty of water sports and fishing, The Riverside Resort is my favorite. It is right on the water and is done up like an old Michigan motel. Great rustic paneled rooms full of games and mini kitchens. Great fun.

In Newaygo is the Log Carpenter. This is one of our best lodge furnishings stores and much of the inventory is actually made by the owner.

SAILOR PINES

SUNRISE WINE AND FOOD FESTIVAL

The Trip:

For just six hours every year some of the best Michigan wine producers, Michigan vineyards and Michigan micro-brewers gather in downtown Harrisville to celebrate with food, music, wine and beer. For fifteen years and counting, those who know come here in July.

On the third Saturday of July, they gather. Fifteen or more vintners will be on hand, several beer brewers and several local restaurants offer up some tasty treats. This has become one of the premier wine-tasting events in the entire Midwest.

What you will find:

Downtown is all dressed up, and soft jazz is played by a live band. You enter the main festival area and begin to graze, wine, cheese and goodies, oh my. A ticket gets you in and a couple of glasses of wine to get you started. After a bit, the harbor will be calling you to stroll along the shore. The N. E. Michigan Art Guild will have a display of local artists to round things out. For a relaxing time in a picturesque village, this is hard to beat. Everyone is in a mellow mood; and everything is right with the world for a time.

Harrisville is one of the most charming towns on the Sunrise Side, in all of Michigan in fact, and this is a very well-attended event. So, if you are planning to stay over, it is best to plan ahead. The Seaver House is an extraordinary B & B, but many of the visiting chefs, vintners and brewers stay there so it may be full.

The Widow's Watch is another great B & B and it is located right across from the harbor. This one, too, is very popular so book your room early. There are a few motels as well but remember that there are also lighthouses, parks, museums etc. so lots of folks are in the area. Rooms do fill quickly this time of year.

Directions:

Harrisville, Michigan, is at the junction of Hwy. 23 and Hwy. 72 south of Thunder Bay and northeast of Iargo Springs. If you run into Lake Huron, you are too far east. If you find Harrisville, you will find the festival.

Side Trips:

The variety of unique shops in this town is remarkable. Let's see, Coming Attractions Gifts, Crafter's Cabin, Moosetales®, Museum Gift Shop and coffee and ice cream and try not to miss the fudge. You can find out about those big Quilt Blocks you see on the barns at the quilt shop downtown, and many a child has caught the first fish ever at the trout farm a few miles north.

MIRROR OF HEAVEN

The Trip:

Kitchitikipi (cold big water) is the largest spring in Michigan at 300 feet by 175 feet. Fed by more than 20 springs, it is refreshed continuously with crystal-clear water. More than 10,000 gallons a minute gush up from the limestone bed.

There are several legends associated with the 40+ foot deep pool. One is that in the past, some of the springs would spout columns of water high into the air.

Another legend may explain the pattern at the bottom of the spring that some say resembles a beautiful native American maiden. While her lover was absent, she was trying to elude an unwanted suitor and dove into the spring. The magical qualities of the waters transformed her into a white deer. From this event came the taboo among native tribes against the killing of white deer.

There are other legends including the idea that the waters were lethal since they don't freeze in winter and no frogs or turtles live in the pool.

What you will find:

The spring is located in Palms Book State Park. There is plenty of parking, and it is an easy walk to the spring along a paved path. There is a State Park fee. While there, you can enjoy a picnic and take advantage of the facilities for a nice rest. A self-operated observation raft guides visitors across the spring so you can view the underwater features and fantasies.

Just past the park entrance is the public access to Indian Lake. Plenty of good fishing is at hand with walleye, bass and pike in abundance.

Directions:

The "Big Spring" Kitch-iti-kipi is located just west of Manistique at Palms Book State Park at the end of M-149. Shop in downtown Manistique, then go across the river where the old siphon bridge is and follow the signs or go west of Manistique on US 2 to Thompson, take M-149 north for 12 miles to the park.

A Little History:

John I. Bellaire, a Manistique businessman, stumbled onto the spring in the early 1900's. He was captivated by the crystal clear pool and watching as the big spring revealed its wonders and fish swam deep in the water. He could have bought the property for himself, but he wanted the spring preserved for all to enjoy. In 1926 he contacted Frank Book of the Palms Book Land Company and the purchase of almost 90 acres of land by the State of Michigan was arranged for $10. The deed requires the property "to be forever used as a public park, bearing the name Palms Book State Park." Additional land has been acquired by the State on Michigan so the park now encompasses 308 acres so the dreams and legends live on.

THE TRILLIUM RAVINE

The Trip:

In deep southwest Michigan, Berrien County is famous for blueberries, wineries, rivers and mills. What is less known, and often overlooked even by the locals, is the park-like Trillium Ravine. Amazingly, this trillium wonderland is just a few miles from Buchanan or Niles; it is easily accessible and is home to a couple of rare wild flowers. The area is a mixed beech-maple woodland; and even though it is now nearly surrounded by a housing development, it is home to two species of toad trilliums at the northern limit of their range, the prairie trillium and a species of wood poppy that only occurs in Michigan's southwestern counties.

What you will find:

Less than a mile from the busy Interstate 31, the 14+acre ravine site is nestled between housing developments that have grown up. As you wind around the roads, you will finally see a small sign announcing the ravine as provided by the Michigan Nature Association. When you enter the forest, it is very open making for an easy walk. There are sugar maples, basswood, ironwood and red oak as well as mature beech trees. By about the first of May, the ground is a riot of wild flowers so thick you can hardly avoid stepping on them. Just a few yards from the road you will find the ravine itself. I estimate it roughly at 150 yards long, 40 yards wide and 20 to 30 feet deep and, the walls are simply covered with trilliums as well as, may apples, trout lily and tons of blue violets. There are narrow pathways so you can wander around without trampling the flowers.

Caution: This is a wild place and the sides of the ravine can be slippery. There is no formal parking lot. The reserve is surrounded by private property. Please respect the boundaries and take out what you take in. Trilliums only bloom for a short time so the trip needs to be late April to mid May.

Directions:

This is tricky because the road names have changed as the area develops. The Walton Rd. runs from Buchanan north and west toward Niles and intersects US 31-33. At that point is a small road Geyer and you want to take it going roughly east. This road will go just a short way into a development and will curve to the right and then take another sharp turn and you find yourself on Riverside Road, just past that point you will cross a small bridge and that is the ravine. There is a small sign.

Side Trips:

Bear Cave – located in nearby Buchanan, this commercial site is the location of a rare lower peninsula waterfall.

LEGEND HAS IT THAT

BANK ROBBERS

HID OUT IN

BEAR CAVE WHILE

ON THE RUN

FROM AN OHIO POSSE

THE TWO TOWERS

The Story:

Travelers heading west from Detroit or east from Chicago still enjoy the "Great Sauk Trail", U.S. 12 and the beautiful Irish Hills. Near Onsted stand two nearly identical towers side by side. They are falling into disrepair these days, but how they came to be is a good story.

In the early 1900's the Irish Hills were just as beautiful and popular as they are today. At that time Cambridge Junction was about as far as you could get on a day trip out of Detroit and still make it back home by dark. Edward Kelly owned land along the road and the Michigan Observation Company wanted to buy a bit of it with the intention of building a viewing tower. Mr. Kelly declined but his neighbor, Edward Brighton, agreed and a 50-foot high tower was built on a high spot and opened in October of 1924. Just in time for folks to travel out, pay five cents, climb to the top and see the spectacular fall colors with brilliant blue lakes scattered throughout.

The new tower was just six feet from the property line and Mr. Kelly was miffed because he thought it obscured the view from his house. To get even, he built a nearly identical tower just 12 feet from the original. What's more he made his tower taller than the original, and the feud was on. The Michigan Observation Company raised their observation platform so it was equal in height to Kelly's "Spite Tower". Further, they let Mr. Kelly know that if this didn't put an end to it, they would tear their tower down and build an enormous steel structure that would dwarf Kelly's. That did it and for several years the competition was in finding unusual ways to attract visitors, even to the point of bringing in alligators and monkeys.

This was a very successful attraction. At one time as many as 50 buses per day were bringing tourists to enjoy the view. The site was open 24 hours per day at one time. The advent of the automobile brought more visitors but also spelled doom for the towers. People could travel further, faster and cheaper and headed for more impressive destinations. By the mid-1960's more than 2 million people had visited the towers. Various problems plagued a series of owners and by the mid-1980's the towers shut down.

What you will find:

While the Irish Hills are as gorgeous as ever, the Towers are pretty sad. It doesn't matter. This is one beautiful area to drive through any time of year.

Directions:

The Towers are near Cambridge Junction where 50 & 12 intersect.

Side Trips:

McCourtie Park is just up the road. It has a stream crossed by 17 bridges. All the work of one artist and all made of concrete.

A QUIET PLACE

The Trip:

A short drive in the country south of Hastings in Barry County, will bring you to 600+ acres of nature trails, wetlands, a kettle lake, constructed prairies and forest lands. The Pierce Cedar Creek Institute is a combination nature area and educational facility. The grounds include seven different trails each of which has its own special characteristics. One trail has wetlands and retention ponds as its main features. Another passes through a fen, an oak forest with huge trees, a pasture/prairie and a view of Brewster Lake. Yet another trail runs through a sand prairie and is characterized by being more primitive than the others. Walkers, hikers, skiers and snowshoe enthusiasts will find a trail that fits their fitness and skill level.

What you will find:

There are spectacular vistas all around and every bit of it is quiet. There are no motorized vehicles here, no snowmobiles, no watercraft, no bicycles, not even any horses; none of them are allowed. There is no fishing, no hunting and no camping, but there is quiet. You can wander through the trees, more than twenty varieties are here from, American Hornbeam to Black Walnut, but collecting is not allowed. Everything is to be enjoyed and preserved. There are wild flowers, wild turkeys and wild deer. There are wild birds as well.

Take the White Trail to the end and relax by the pure running water of the river. On the east loop of the Blue Trail, the observant can spot a beech tree with branches that actually form a closed loop. Further on is the recently added boardwalk through a wetland.

The wild and beautiful nature areas are augmented by the educational facility. Visitors can learn about restoring and preserving natural habitats, select educational materials about Michigan and its wildlife, and enjoy the programs held in these earth friendly buildings. Information is available on bird and butterfly gardening, prairie management, wildlife tracking, the solstices and much more. Then, it is back out into the sunshine for a walk through nature itself and the pure enjoyment of a quiet place. The institute is open all four seasons.

Directions:

The Pierce Cedar Creek Institute is on Cloverdale Rd. near Hastings in Barry County. M-37 runs from Grand Rapids to Battle Creek. Cloverdale Rd. is about midway and is actually disconnected east and west. You want to take the branch that goes west from M-37. It is a gravel road that winds through the country and wetlands and brings you to the institute. There is plenty of paved parking, and the trails are well marked.

Side Trips:

Another favorite of nature lovers is the Baker Sanctuary in nearby Eaton County outside Bellevue. It is the site of the Sandhill Crane Festival every October.

The Dowling General Store on Route 37 is not to be missed.

TRIP NOTES

TRIP NOTES

TRIP NOTES

TRIP NOTES

TRIP NOTES

TRIP NOTES

TRIP NOTES

TRIP NOTES

TRIP NOTES

TRIP NOTES

TRIP NOTES

TRIP NOTES

TRIP NOTES